Cryptocurrency Investing Book 2024

Beginner's Guide towards successful Cryptocurrency investment in 2024

BY
Pete Dan

Table of Contents

Ethereum and the Rise of Smart Contracts

CHAPTER ONE

INTRODUCTION

You are most welcome to the dynamic realm of cryptocurrency investing, a space where traditional finance meets cutting-edge technology, and fortunes can be made or lost in the blink of an eye. As we journey into the year 2024, the landscape of digital assets has evolved, presenting both opportunities and challenges that demand a nuanced understanding.

Cryptocurrency, which stemmed from the decentralised vision of Bitcoin's pseudonymous creator Satoshi Nakamoto in 2009, has since burgeoned into a diverse ecosystem. It's no longer just about Bitcoin; altcoins, tokens, and decentralised finance (DeFi) projects have proliferated, offering a myriad of investment avenues. The market's metamorphosis has invited both seasoned investors and newcomers, drawn by the promise of financial revolution.

Our journey into cryptocurrency investing unravels against the backdrop of a rapidly changing financial paradigm. Imagine a world where traditional banks no longer hold a monopoly on transactions, and value transfer occurs seamlessly across borders. Envision decentralised applications reshaping industries, enabling peer-to-peer transactions without intermediaries. This is the promise and potential of cryptocurrencies.

To guide you through this digital frontier, our narrative begins with a protagonist whose name is Melvin. A tech-savvy individual with an appetite for risk, Melvin represents the new breed of investors navigating the volatile waves of the cryptocurrency market. His journey encompasses the excitement, challenges, and triumphs that await those venturing into this captivating realm.

As Melvin delves into cryptocurrency investing, he encounters the foundational pillar of this space – blockchain technology. At its core, blockchain is a decentralised and immutable ledger that underpins most cryptocurrencies. Its transparent and secure nature has far-reaching implications, not only for financial transactions but also for sectors like supply chain, healthcare, and governance.

The introduction of smart contracts, self-executing contracts with the terms of the agreement directly written into code, further enhances the capabilities of blockchain. This innovation powers the burgeoning DeFi movement, where individuals can engage in lending, borrowing, and trading without traditional financial intermediaries. Alex witnesses the disruptive potential of these decentralized applications, challenging the status quo of traditional finance.

Yet, amidst the promises of innovation, Melvin grapples with the inherent volatility of the cryptocurrency market. Prices can soar to dizzying heights, only to plummet precipitously. The market's susceptibility to speculation, regulatory developments, and technological advancements makes it a rollercoaster ride for investors. Our narrative explores risk management strategies and the importance of thorough research in navigating these turbulent waters.

As Melvin encounters various cryptocurrencies – from the stalwarts like Bitcoin and Ethereum to the up-and-coming altcoins – he learns to discern between genuine innovations and fleeting trends. The importance of due diligence, understanding the technology behind each project, and evaluating the team's credibility become crucial factors in his investment decisions.

Our exploration extends beyond the digital realm as Melvin confronts the regulatory landscape shaping cryptocurrency markets. Governments worldwide grapple with how to regulate and integrate these digital assets into existing financial frameworks. The interplay between innovation and regulation adds another layer of complexity to the evolving narrative of cryptocurrency investing.

In this book, we aim to provide a comprehensive guide to cryptocurrency investing, blending theoretical knowledge with practical insights drawn from real-world experiences. Whether you're a seasoned investor seeking to adapt your strategies to the changing landscape or a newcomer navigating this brave new world, our narrative promises to be your trusted companion in the exciting journey of cryptocurrency investing in 2024.

CHAPTER TWO
Foundation of Cryptocurrency

Blockchain Technology

Blockchain is a decentralised, transparent ledger system powering cryptocurrencies and various applications. Comprising interconnected blocks, each containing transaction data, it employs cryptographic hashes for secure, tamper-proof linkages. Transactions are verified by a network of nodes through consensus mechanisms, ensuring data integrity without a central authority. Beyond cryptocurrencies, blockchain's distributed and trustless nature is revolutionising industries, offering transparent and secure solutions for processes ranging from supply chain management to financial transactions, reshaping how data is stored, verified, and exchanged.

Smart Contracts

Smart contracts are self-executing contracts with coded terms, running on blockchain technology. These automated agreements facilitate, verify, or enforce the negotiation or performance of a contract. Built on decentralized platforms like Ethereum, they operate without intermediaries, executing actions when predefined conditions are met. Smart contracts enhance transparency, reduce fraud, and streamline processes across various industries, from finance to real estate.

Decentralised Applications (DApps)

Decentralised Applications (DApps) are applications running on a blockchain, ensuring decentralised control and often utilising smart contracts. Unlike traditional apps, DApps operate on a peer-to-peer network, removing single points of failure and enhancing security. They span various domains such as finance (DeFi), gaming, and social networking, offering users greater autonomy and data ownership. DApps represent a key element in the broader blockchain ecosystem, embodying the principles of decentralisation and transparency in software development.

CHAPTER THREE

**Navigating the
Cryptocurrency Market**

Risk Management Techniques in Cryptocurrency

It is important to state here that for one to ensure successful cryptocurrency trading in 2024, he should take cognizance of the following techniques in managing risks associated with cryptocurrency. They include but not limited to the following;

1. **Diversification:** To lower risk, distribute your money among several cryptocurrencies. In this manner, losses from a failing asset may be balanced by gains from others.

2. **Research and Analysis:** Keep up with news, technological advancements, and market trends related to cryptocurrencies. Performing in-depth research can assist you in making wise investment choices.

3. **Put Stop-Loss Orders in Place:** Use stop-loss orders to have cryptocurrencies automatically sold when their price hits a certain threshold. This reduces the amount that could be lost during market downturns.

4. **Employ Cold Wallets:** Put a large percentage of your cryptocurrency holdings in cold storage or hardware wallets. Your valuables are shielded from online hacking attempts by doing this.

5. **Risk Assessment:** Consider the level of risk attached to every coin. When making investment decisions, take into account variables including volatility, liquidity, and regulatory developments

The Role of Research in Investment Decisions

Research plays a pivotal role in cryptocurrency investment resources, guiding investors through the complex and dynamic landscape of digital assets. In the realm of cryptocurrencies, where markets are highly volatile and sentiment-driven, informed decision-making is crucial. Comprehensive research empowers investors to navigate risks, seize opportunities, and make strategic choices.

Fundamental analysis is key in assessing the long-term viability of a cryptocurrency. Investigating the project's whitepaper, development team, and underlying technology helps investors gauge the potential for sustained growth. Understanding the utility and real-world applications of a cryptocurrency provides valuable insights into its future prospects.

Technical analysis complements fundamental research by examining historical price data and market trends.

Analyzing charts and identifying patterns assists investors in making more informed predictions about future price movements. Technical indicators and chart patterns can be instrumental in timing entry and exit points, optimising returns.

Moreover, staying abreast of regulatory developments is essential. Cryptocurrency markets are susceptible to regulatory changes, and research enables investors to anticipate and adapt to evolving legal landscapes. Assessing the regulatory environment enhances risk management and compliance.

Community sentiment is another critical aspect. Monitoring social media channels, forums, and community discussions provides a pulse on market sentiment. Recognizing shifts in public perception can be a leading indicator of potential market movements.

Continuous learning is imperative in the cryptocurrency space, given its rapid evolution. Researching emerging technologies, trends, and market dynamics helps investors stay ahead of the curve. Accessing reputable news sources, industry reports, and expert analyses contributes to a well-rounded understanding of the market.

In conclusion, research serves as the foundation for sound decision-making in cryptocurrency investments. By combining fundamental and technical analyses, staying informed on regulatory developments, monitoring community sentiment, and engaging in continuous learning, investors can navigate the complexities of the cryptocurrency market with greater confidence and success.

CHAPTER FOUR

Cryptocurrencies: Beyond Bitcoin

Ethereum and the Rise of Smart Contracts

The 2015 debut of Ethereum by Vitalik Buterin marks a revolutionary advancement in blockchain technology. Ethereum is not just a digital currency, in contrast to its forerunner, Bitcoin. It presented the idea of smart contracts, which are self-executing agreements with the conditions of the contract explicitly encoded into the code. Numerous sectors have been significantly impacted by this breakthrough.

Decentralised apps, or DApps, are the means by which smart contracts on the Ethereum blockchain provide automated and programmable transactions devoid of middlemen. Compared to traditional methods, this decentralised method improves efficiency, security, and transparency.

The Ethereum Virtual Machine (EVM), a runtime environment for smart contracts, is one of the main features of Ethereum. Developers have the ability to construct a wide range of apps, such as non-fungible

Exploring Altcoins and Their Unique Features

Altcoins, or alternative cryptocurrencies to Bitcoin, have surged in popularity and diversity since the inception of blockchain technology. As Bitcoin remains the pioneer and dominant cryptocurrency, altcoins aim to offer unique features and improvements, catering to specific niches within the crypto ecosystem. Exploring the vast landscape of altcoins reveals a rich tapestry of innovation, each with its distinctive features.

One notable category of altcoins includes privacy-focused cryptocurrencies. Coins like Monero, Zcash, and Dash implement advanced cryptographic techniques to ensure enhanced privacy and anonymity in transactions. By utilising technologies like ring signatures and zero-knowledge proofs, these altcoins aim to address the privacy concerns often associated with traditional cryptocurrencies. Users seeking increased confidentiality are drawn to these alternatives.

Smart contract platforms represent another significant segment of altcoins. Ethereum, often considered the pioneer in this domain, introduced the concept of programmable contracts that execute automatically when predefined conditions are met. Competitors like Binance Smart Chain, Cardano, and Solana have entered the scene, each with its approach to scalability, security, and interoperability. These platforms enable developers to create decentralised applications (DApps) and smart contracts, fostering a robust ecosystem of decentralised finance (DeFi) and non-fungible tokens (NFTs).

Stablecoins, pegged to the value of traditional fiat currencies, form a crucial part of the altcoin market. Tether (USDT), USD Coin (USDC), and DAI are examples of stablecoins that offer stability and liquidity, serving as a bridge between the volatile crypto market and traditional finance. These coins play a vital role in facilitating trading, providing a relatively stable store of value, and supporting various financial applications within the crypto space.

Some altcoins focus on environmental sustainability, addressing concerns about the energy consumption associated with traditional proof-of-work consensus mechanisms. Coins like Cardano and Algorand utilise proof-of-stake or other energy-efficient consensus algorithms, aiming to reduce their carbon footprint. This eco-friendly approach appeals to users and investors increasingly conscious of the environmental impact of blockchain technology.

In the realm of interoperability, altcoins like Polkadot and Cosmos aim to facilitate communication and collaboration between different blockchains. These projects strive to overcome the issue of isolated blockchain networks by enabling seamless transfer of assets and data across diverse platforms. Interoperability is seen as a key factor in achieving the widespread adoption of blockchain technology and fostering a more interconnected decentralised ecosystem.

Altcoins also explore niche use cases and industries. For instance, Chain Link focuses on decentralised oracle services, enabling smart contracts to interact with real-world data. VeChain targets supply chain management, utilising blockchain to enhance transparency and traceability in product supply chains. These specialised altcoins demonstrate the versatility of blockchain technology in addressing specific challenges across various sectors.

In conclusion, exploring altcoins unveils a diverse landscape of cryptocurrencies, each designed to address specific challenges or cater to unique user preferences. Whether prioritising privacy, scalability, sustainability, or niche applications, altcoins contribute to the evolution of the crypto space. As the ecosystem continues to mature, the interplay between Bitcoin and these alternative cryptocurrencies will shape the future of decentralised finance, governance, and innovation.

CHAPTER FIVE

Decentralised Finance (DeFi)

Decentralised Finance (DeFi) represents a revolutionary shift in the traditional financial landscape by leveraging blockchain technology to create an open and decentralised ecosystem of financial services. In essence, DeFi aims to eliminate the need for traditional intermediaries like banks and brokers, allowing users to engage in financial activities directly through decentralised applications (DApps) on blockchain platforms, predominantly Ethereum.

One key aspect of DeFi is smart contracts, self-executing contracts with the terms of the agreement directly written into code. These smart contracts automate various financial functions, such as lending, borrowing, and trading, providing a transparent and trustless environment. Decentralised exchanges (DEXs) are central to DeFi, allowing users to trade cryptocurrencies without relying on a centralised authority, enhancing security and reducing counterparty risk.

Lending and borrowing platforms within the DeFi space enable users to lend their assets and earn interest or borrow assets by providing collateral. This process is facilitated by smart contracts, ensuring the integrity of transactions. Decentralised autonomous organisations (DAOs) are another significant component, enabling community-driven governance and decision-making in DeFi protocols.

While DeFi holds great promise, challenges persist, including security vulnerabilities, regulatory uncertainties, and scalability issues. Nonetheless, its rapid growth demonstrates a hunger for financial inclusivity and a desire to reshape the traditional financial system. As the DeFi space continues to evolve, addressing these challenges will be crucial to realising its full potential and ensuring a more accessible and equitable financial future

The DeFi Movement

The goal of the blockchain-based financial system known as Decentralised Finance (DeFi) is to replicate existing financial services without the use of conventional middlemen like banks. Key elements of the DeFi movement are as follows:

Decentralisation: Ethereum and other blockchain technologies serve as the foundation for DeFi's decentralised networks. This promotes transparency and lowers the possibility of censorship by guaranteeing that there is no single entity in charge of the system.

Smart contracts are self-executing agreements that have the terms encoded directly into the code. These are employed in DeFi to automate a range of financial operations, eliminating the need for middlemen in the lending, borrowing, and trading processes.

Decentralised lending and borrowing services: Decentralised lending and borrowing services are provided by DeFi platforms through their lending and borrowing protocols. Users can borrow assets by supplying or lending their bitcoin assets to earn interest.

Stablecoins: In order to give DeFi a steady unit of account, stablecoins backed by fiat money or real assets are essential. Examples of stable values that are maintained through algorithmic control or collateralization are USDC, USDT, and DAI.

Decentralised Autonomous Organizations (DAOs): DAOs are groups of people who decide how to operate together and are controlled by smart contracts. DAOs are utilised in DeFi's decision-making procedures to provide users a voice in the creation and management of the platforms.

Liquidity mining and yield farming allow users to gain more tokens by giving DeFi platforms liquidity. In order to accommodate different protocols, assets are locked up in smart contracts through a process called yield farming, often referred to as liquidity mining, in exchange for more tokens.

Cross-Chain DeFi: As interoperability becomes more important, assets can transfer between blockchains with ease. The goal of projects like Cosmos and Polkadot is to make transactions and communication between various blockchain networks easier.

Dangers and Difficulties: There are various dangers associated with DeFi, such as regulatory uncertainties, market volatility, and weaknesses in smart contracts. Users must evaluate the dangers connected to each DeFi protocol carefully.

The DeFi movement has gotten a lot of popularity, giving people more access to financial resources, less dependence on traditional banks, and fresh chances for financial industry innovation. However, given DeFi's developing nature and potential concerns, it's imperative to approach the technology cautiously and thoroughly research it.

Lending, Borrowing, and Trading without Intermediaries.

By utilising blockchain technology to build decentralised financial institutions, the DeFi movement signifies a paradigm shift in the conventional financial environment. Lending, borrowing, and trading without the need for conventional middlemen are essential elements.

1. **Lending**: Using DeFi systems, individuals can lend their digital assets in an autonomous way. Blockchain-powered smart contracts replace traditional banks by automating loan procedures. While borrowers obtain capital without undergoing conventional credit checks, lenders receive interest on their holdings.

2. **Borrowing:** By enabling peer-to-peer lending, DeFi gives consumers access to money without the need of banks or other lending organizations.

Smart contracts guarantee security and transparency by enforcing agreements. The ability of borrowers to pledge their cryptocurrency holdings as security fosters a climate of trustless lending.

3. **Trading:** At the heart of DeFi trading are decentralised exchanges, or DEXs. Users can trade different cryptocurrencies directly while keeping total control over their money. By doing away with the requirement for centralised exchanges, counterparty risk is decreased and transaction security is raised overall.

4. **Intermediary-Free Ecosystem:** The DeFi movement is based on the idea that there should be no middlemen. By automating procedures, blockchain technology and smart contracts lessen dependency on conventional financial institutions. Disintermediation democratises access to financial services, lowers prices, and improves efficiency.

5. **Risks and Challenges:** Although DeFi offers novel solutions, there are hazards associated with it. Challenges include market volatility, regulatory concerns, and weaknesses in smart contracts. To allay these worries, security audits and effective risk management are crucial.

6. **Tokenization:** This is a common component of DeFi, in which tokens on the blockchain reflect real-world assets. This makes fractional ownership, more liquidity, and wider investor accessibility possible.

7. **Governance and Decentralization:** Decentralised

governance methods are a feature of many DeFi projects. By actively participating in decision-making processes, token holders can influence the platform's future. The goal of this decentralised strategy is to develop financial ecosystems that are more inclusive and community-driven.

In summary, the DeFi movement is a revolutionary step toward a transparent, inclusive, and decentralised financial system. Without middlemen, lending, borrowing, and trading give consumers more power and provide reliable, accessible, and efficient financial services. Nevertheless, obstacles still exist, requiring constant innovation and strong risk management to guarantee the DeFi ecosystem's long-term viability.

CHAPTER SIX

The Risk and Reward: Tales from the Cryptocurrency Market

Success Stories

Cryptocurrency markets are a dynamic landscape where risk and reward coexist, offering tales of both triumph and tribulation. Success stories in this realm are often characterised by individuals who navigated the volatile market with strategic acumen. Investors who entered the scene early, such as those who bought Bitcoin in its nascent stages, witnessed unprecedented rewards as the cryptocurrency soared in value over the years.

On the other hand, risk is inherent in the cryptocurrency market, with price fluctuations and regulatory uncertainties posing constant challenges. However, some success stories emerge from those who skillfully managed these risks. Traders employing technical analysis, fundamental research, and risk management strategies have been able to capitalise on market trends, turning potential pitfalls into opportunities.

Notable tales include those who identified and invested in promising altcoins before they gained widespread attention, reaping substantial returns. Additionally, successful projects and ICOs (Initial Coin Offerings) have spawned stories of early backers becoming millionaires as the projects matured.

However, cautionary tales exist too, underscoring the importance of thorough research and prudent decision-making. The cryptocurrency market's decentralised nature adds to its allure but demands a keen understanding of the risks involved.

In conclusion, the risk and reward dynamics in the cryptocurrency market offer a rich tapestry of success stories. These narratives showcase the potential for substantial gains, often accompanied by the need for savvy risk management. The cryptocurrency market remains a fascinating arena where fortunes can be made or lost, providing valuable insights for aspiring investors.

Lesson from failures in Cryptocurrency

Failures in the cryptocurrency space serve as instructive lessons for both seasoned investors and newcomers. The market's notorious volatility and susceptibility to external factors emphasize the importance of comprehensive research and risk management. Instances of failed projects, fraudulent schemes, and regulatory crackdowns underscore the need for due diligence before investing. These setbacks highlight the unpredictable nature of the cryptocurrency landscape and the necessity for adaptability in navigating unforeseen challenges. Learning from these failures encourages a cautious approach, fostering a more resilient and informed investor community. Ultimately, acknowledging and analysing failures in the cryptocurrency realm contributes to a collective understanding that can mitigate risks and pave the way for a more sustainable and mature market.

CHAPTER SEVEN

Regulatory Landscape

Governments and Cryptocurrency Regulation

Governments around the world have grappled with the emergence of cryptocurrencies, attempting to strike a balance between embracing innovation and safeguarding financial systems. The regulatory landscape for cryptocurrencies varies significantly, reflecting the diverse perspectives and approaches adopted by different countries.

Some nations have embraced cryptocurrencies, recognizing their potential for economic growth and technological advancement. Others, however, have taken a more cautious stance, expressing concerns about the potential for illicit activities such as money laundering and fraud associated with digital currencies. Regulatory frameworks often focus on key areas such as consumer protection, anti-money laundering (AML), and combating the financing of terrorism (CFT).

In countries like Japan and Switzerland, there has been a proactive effort to integrate cryptocurrencies into existing financial systems, with clear regulatory frameworks in place. In contrast, China has implemented strict measures, including bans on initial coin offerings (ICOs) and cryptocurrency exchanges, aiming to maintain control over its financial system.

The United States has adopted a nuanced approach, with various regulatory bodies overseeing different aspects of the cryptocurrency space. The Commodity Futures Trading Commission (CFTC) views certain cryptocurrencies as commodities, while the Securities and Exchange Commission (SEC) regulates those deemed securities.

The European Union has sought to create a unified approach through initiatives like the Markets in Crypto-Assets Regulation (MiCA), aiming to provide legal clarity and foster innovation while mitigating risks.

As the cryptocurrency ecosystem continues to evolve, governments face the ongoing challenge of adapting regulations to address emerging technologies and ensure the stability and security of financial markets.

Impact on Markets and Investors

Government regulations play a pivotal role in shaping the cryptocurrency market and influencing investor behaviour. The impact can be both positive and negative, depending on the regulatory framework implemented by authorities. On the positive side, clear regulations can provide a sense of legitimacy to the cryptocurrency space, attracting institutional investors who may have been hesitant due to concerns about legal uncertainties. This increased institutional participation often leads to greater market stability and liquidity.

Conversely, overly restrictive regulations or sudden regulatory changes can create uncertainty and volatility in the cryptocurrency market. Investors may become wary, and market sentiment can be adversely affected. Governments also have the power to influence the value of cryptocurrencies through policy decisions, such as bans on trading or mining activities.

Furthermore, regulatory actions aimed at protecting consumers and preventing illegal activities in the crypto space can enhance investor confidence. However, striking the right balance between fostering innovation and safeguarding investors is a complex challenge for governments.

Global coordination on cryptocurrency regulations is another critical factor, as the decentralised nature of cryptocurrencies often transcends national borders. Divergent regulatory approaches among countries can create challenges for cross-border transactions and hinder the growth of the overall market.

In conclusion, government and regulatory interventions significantly shape the landscape for cryptocurrency investors. Well-crafted regulations can foster a healthy and sustainable market, while poorly implemented or inconsistent regulations may hinder its development and pose risks to investors. Achieving a balance that encourages innovation while safeguarding investors remains a key challenge for regulators worldwide.

.

CHAPTER EIGHT

The Future of Cryptocurrency

Technological Advancement in the Horizon

The future of cryptocurrency promises intriguing technological advances.

Blockchain, the backbone of cryptocurrencies, may witness enhanced scalability and interoperability solutions, addressing current limitations. Smart contracts, self-executing contracts with coded terms, are likely to evolve, enabling more complex and automated transactions. Privacy-focused cryptocurrencies may gain prominence, incorporating advanced encryption techniques. Central Bank Digital Currencies (CBDCs) could become widespread, revolutionising traditional finance. Additionally, advancements in quantum computing may challenge existing cryptographic protocols, prompting the development of quantum-resistant solutions. As the crypto landscape evolves, regulatory frameworks will likely adapt, shaping the trajectory of this transformative financial ecosystem.

Shaping the Next Era of Finance

Cryptocurrency stands at the van of shaping the coming period of finance, steering in a paradigm shift in how we perceive and engage with traditional financial systems. Decentralisation lies at the heart of cryptocurrencies, challenging the centralised control exercised by traditional fiscal institutions. Blockchain technology, the beginning foundation of utmost cryptocurrencies, ensures translucency, security, and invariability in deals. The rise of cryptocurrencies has normalised fiscal access, enabling people around the globe to share in the fiscal ecosystem without the need for interposers. This fiscal inclusivity has the implicit to hoist unbanked populations, furnishing them with avenues for savings, investments, and profitable participation. Smart contracts, a crucial point of blockchain technology, automate and apply contractual agreements, reducing the need for interposers and streamlining processes. This not only enhances effectiveness but also minimises the threat of fraud. Still, the transformative power of cryptocurrencies isn't without challenges. Regulatory misgivings, volatility, and scalability issues pose hurdles to mainstream relinquishment. Striking a balance between invention and regulation becomes pivotal to icing the responsible elaboration of the cryptocurrency geography. As cryptocurrencies continue to evolve, their impact on the fiscal sector will probably extend beyond borders, impacting global trade, remittances, and investment practices. The ongoing integration of cryptocurrencies into mainstream fiscal systems marks a vital moment in the ongoing narrative of finance, promising a more inclusive, effective, and decentralised future.

CHAPTER NINE

PRACTICAL GUIDELINES FOR INVESTORS

Building a Cryptocurrency Portfolio

Erecting a cryptocurrency portfolio requires a strategic approach to alleviate pitfalls and optimize returns. Then are practical guidelines for investors to consider when venturing into the unpredictable world of cryptocurrencies.

1.:Diversification: This is crucial to get optimum results, you have to spread your investments across multiple cryptocurrencies to reduce threats. Avoid putting all your finances into one asset, as the cryptocurrency request is largely changeable. Diversification can help cover your portfolio from the extreme volatility frequently associated with individual coins.

2. Research Completely ahead investing, conduct comprehensive exploration on the cryptocurrencies you are interested in. dissect the technology, use case, development platoon, and community support. Understand the request trends and implicit challenges. Informed opinions are pivotal in this dynamic request.

3. Understand Risk Tolerance Assess your threat forbearance before entering

the request. Cryptocurrency prices can be largely unpredictable, and values may witness significant oscillations. ensure that your threat forbearance aligns with the implicit ups and campo of the request to avoid making emotional, impulsive opinions.

4. Keep Abreast of Market Trends Stay streamlined on request trends and news related to the cryptocurrency space. Changes in regulations, technological advancements, or significant hookups can impact the value of your investments. Regularly cover dependable news sources and social media channels to stay informed.

5. Secure Your Investments Implement robust security measures to cover your cryptocurrency effects. Use tackle holdalls for secure software holdalls with two- factor authentication. Be conservative about participating in particular information and be apprehensive of phishing attempts. Security is consummate in the crypto space.

6. Long- Term Perspective Cryptocurrency requests can be largely unpredictable in the short term. Consider espousing a long- term investment strategy to ride out request oscillations. tolerance is crucial in the crypto space, as long- term investors frequently see more significant returns.

7. Stay Sceptical of Hype Be cautious of exorbitantly hyped systems or unrealistic pledges. Due industriousness is pivotal, and investments should be grounded on substance rather than hype. Guard of pump- and- leave schemes and exorbitantly auspicious

claims that may not be backed by solid fundamentals.

8. Monitor Portfolio Regularly Regularly review and rebalance your cryptocurrency portfolio grounded on request conditions and your investment pretensions. Reassess the performance of each asset and make adaptations if demanded. This active operation approach can help optimise your portfolio over time.

9. Consider Regulatory Environment Be apprehensive of the nonsupervisory terrain girding cryptocurrencies in your governance. Regulations can impact the request and the legitimacy of certain conditioning. Stay biddable with original laws to avoid legal issues that could peril your investments.

10. Seek Professional Advice still, consider seeking advice from fiscal professionals who specialise in digital means, If you are uncertain about certain aspects of cryptocurrency investing. Their moxie can give precious perceptivity and guidance acclimatised to your individual situation. In conclusion, erecting a cryptocurrency portfolio demands a combination of exploration, threat operation, and a chastened approach. By following these practical guidelines, investors can navigate the complications of the cryptocurrency request with lesser confidence and increase the liability of achieving their fiscal objectives.

Tools and Platforms for Trading and Analysis

Tools and platforms for trading and analysis have undergone significant advancements in recent years, reshaping the landscape of financial markets. As technology continues to evolve, traders and investors now have access to a diverse array of sophisticated tools and platforms designed to enhance decision-making, streamline execution, and provide comprehensive market analysis.

One of the key elements in the arsenal of a modern trader is the trading platform. These platforms serve as the interface between the trader and the financial markets, offering real-time market data, order execution capabilities, and various analytical tools. Popular examples include MetaTrader 4 (MT4), thinkorswim, and TradingView. MT4, a widely used platform, is known for its user-friendly interface and extensive library of technical analysis tools. thinkorswim, offered by TD Ameritrade, provides advanced charting and analysis tools, while TradingView stands out for its social collaboration features, allowing users to share charts and ideas with a global community.

Analytical tools play a crucial role in empowering traders with insights into market trends and potential opportunities. Technical analysis tools, such as moving averages, RSI, and Fibonacci retracement, help traders identify price patterns and make informed decisions. Fundamental analysis tools, on the other hand, focus on assessing the intrinsic value of an asset based on economic indicators, financial reports, and market trends. Bloomberg Terminal is a renowned example, offering a comprehensive suite of tools for both technical and fundamental analysis, coupled with real-time news and financial data.

Algorithmic trading has gained prominence with the rise of automated strategies and machine learning. Algorithmic trading platforms enable traders to execute pre-defined strategies automatically, based on specific criteria or signals. QuantConnect and AlgoTrader are examples of platforms catering to algorithmic traders. These platforms provide backtesting capabilities, allowing users to evaluate the performance of their strategies using historical data before deploying them in live markets.

In recent years, the emergence of cryptocurrencies has introduced new trading platforms tailored to digital assets. Exchanges like Binance and Coinbase offer user-friendly interfaces for buying, selling, and trading cryptocurrencies. Additionally, decentralised finance (DeFi) platforms, built on blockchain technology, provide opportunities for decentralised trading, lending, and yield farming.

Risk management tools are integral for traders seeking to protect their capital. Stop-loss orders, margin management features, and risk-reward calculators help traders define and control their risk exposure.

Advanced platforms like Interactive Brokers and eToro provide robust risk management tools alongside their trading functionalities.

Social trading platforms have transformed the way individuals approach investing. Platforms like eToro and ZuluTrade enable users to follow the trades of experienced investors, allowing for a collaborative and educational approach to trading. This social aspect fosters a sense of community and knowledge-sharing among users.

The evolution of trading and analysis tools also extends to mobile applications. Mobile trading apps offered by brokerage firms allow users to monitor markets, execute trades, and access research on the go. These apps, such as Robinhood and E*TRADE, have democratised access to financial markets by providing a user-friendly experience on mobile devices.

In conclusion, the landscape of tools and platforms for trading and analysis has become diverse and sophisticated, catering to the evolving needs of traders and investors. From traditional stock markets to cryptocurrencies and decentralised finance, the tools available today empower individuals with unprecedented access to information and execution capabilities, revolutionising the way financial markets are navigated and understood.

CHAPTER TEN

CONCLUSION

REFLECTION ON THE CRYPTOCURRENCY JOURNEY

The cryptocurrency journey has been a rollercoaster of innovation, speculation, and regulatory scrutiny. Emerging from the shadows of anonymity, cryptocurrencies challenged traditional financial systems, promising decentralised, borderless transactions. Bitcoin, the pioneer, sparked a revolution, attracting both enthusiasts and sceptics. Price volatility became synonymous with the crypto market, offering substantial gains but also posing risks. As governments grappled with regulatory frameworks, debates intensified over the role of cryptocurrencies in the global economy. Amidst technological advancements like blockchain, the community faced scalability and sustainability concerns. NFTs (Non-Fungible Tokens) brought a new dimension to digital ownership. Reflecting on this journey reveals a sector in constant evolution, navigating the delicate balance between innovation and stability. The resilience of cryptocurrencies has spurred dialogue on financial inclusivity, privacy, and the future of money. As the landscape continues to mature, the cryptocurrency journey remains a testament to the transformative power of decentralised technologies.

Looking Ahead to 2025

As we approach 2025, the cryptocurrency landscape is poised for significant developments. The relentless evolution of blockchain technology continues to drive innovation, paving the way for new possibilities in decentralised finance (DeFi), non-fungible tokens (NFTs), and beyond.

In the coming years, scalability and sustainability will be focal points. Scalability solutions, such as layer 2 protocols and sharding, aim to address the inherent challenges of transaction speed and cost within blockchain networks. Additionally, the industry is likely to witness increased collaboration between traditional finance and crypto, leading to further integration and mainstream adoption.

Regulatory frameworks are anticipated to mature, providing clearer guidelines for market participants. This regulatory clarity could attract institutional investors seeking a more secure and compliant environment. Interoperability between different blockchain networks is also gaining attention, fostering greater connectivity and fluidity in the decentralised ecosystem.

Moreover, advancements in privacy-focused technologies and consensus algorithms may redefine the balance between transparency and confidentiality within blockchain networks. As the metaverse gains traction, cryptocurrencies could play a pivotal role in shaping virtual economies and transactions within digital realms.

In summary, the outlook for 2025 in cryptocurrency is characterised by technological refinement, regulatory evolution, and increased collaboration, setting the stage for a dynamic and transformative era in the world of digital assets.